Poppin Beans

by Deborah Lynne Younger-Mitchell

Extreme Overflow Publishing
Grayson, GA USA

Extreme Overflow Publishing
A brand of Extreme Overflow Enterprises, Inc.
P.O. Box 1184
Grayson, GA 30017
For bulk orders visit: www.extremeoverflow.com

Send feedback to:
info@extreme-overflow-enterprises.com

Printed in the United State of America

Editing by Extreme Overflow Publishing
Book Cover and Layout by Extreme Overflow Publishing

Library of Congress Catalogin-Publication Data is available for this title.

ISBN: 978-0-9976256-0-8

Acknowledgements

I would like to thank my Lord and Saviour Jesus Christ. I would like to thank my dad, James Melvin Younger, I who encouraged me to keep writing my story. I would also like to thank my mother, Margaret Anne Younger who also encouraged me and told me that I had several children's books inside of me. I want to thank Leah Elizabeth Mitchell, my daughter who is my inspiration to write and to pass on family legacies. I want to thank all of my siblings, cousins, nieces, nephews and aunts and uncles for their encouragement. I want to thank my grandmother Barbara A. Irving affectionately called Nana, for her prayers and encouragement. I want to thank all of my elders that have gone on before me; my grandparents, Alphonso C. and Maggie C. Irving and Rufus H. Younger, Sr. and Mary M. Younger who without them sharing their teachings and stories, there would be no Poppin Beans. Thank you to Extreme Overflow Publishing for making my vision come alive.

Dedication

This book is dedicated to my daughter Leah Elizabeth Mitchell.

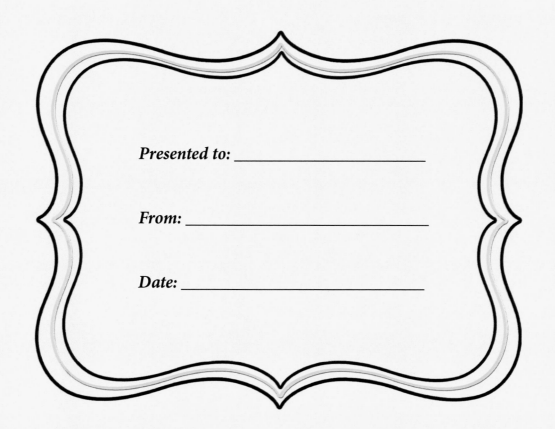

Presented to: _____

From: _____

Date: _____

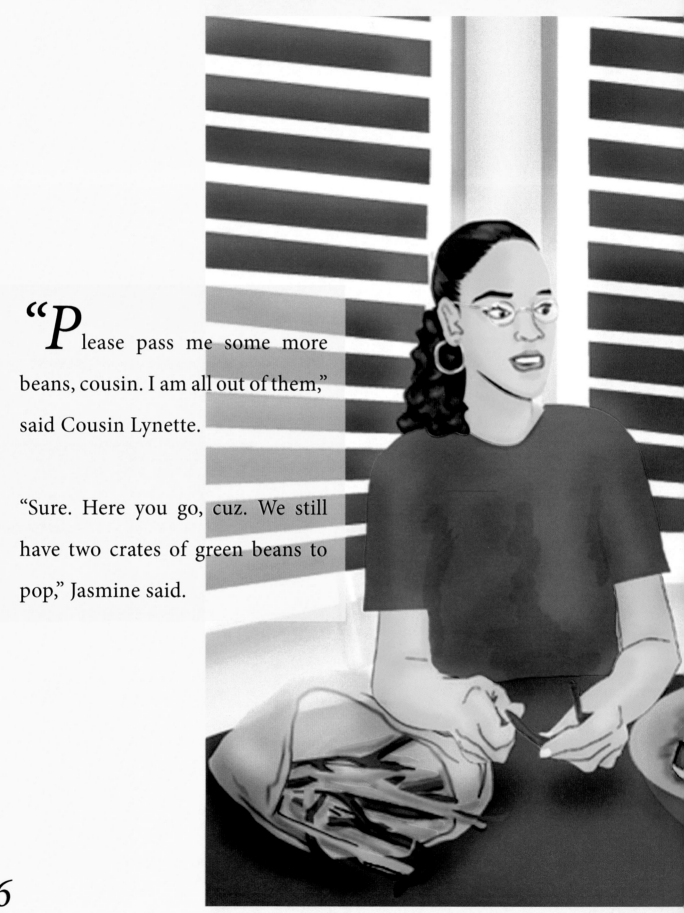

"Please pass me some more beans, cousin. I am all out of them," said Cousin Lynette.

"Sure. Here you go, cuz. We still have two crates of green beans to pop," Jasmine said.

6

Jasmine and her cousin Lynette sat at the kitchen table popping beans for their Great Aunt Mary's home going celebration taking place the next day.

'This is going to take all night,' Jasmine thought as she stared at the crates of string beans next to the refrigerator. Jasmine had already snapped so many beans that her hands began to turn green. But she was so happy to help and be together with her loved ones.

*I*t was especially warm that sunny May afternoon. There were clusters of family in every area of the house. Aunt Maggie was in the living room with children gathered around her listening to the amazing way she told the great stories of the bible. Since childhood Jasmine loved Aunt Maggie's bible lessons. One of her favorite stories was the one about Joseph and his brothers because she too was a dreamer like Joseph.

On that warm sunny day before Great Aunt Mary's home going celebration there were lots of children in the backyard playing tag. There were even younger ones playing on the jungle gym allowing them to be in a world all to themselves.

12

There were rambunctious boys playing soccer. And of course there were lots of towering teens all huddled together - talking their lingo, laughing and sharing what happened on the latest episode of the cable TV shows.

13

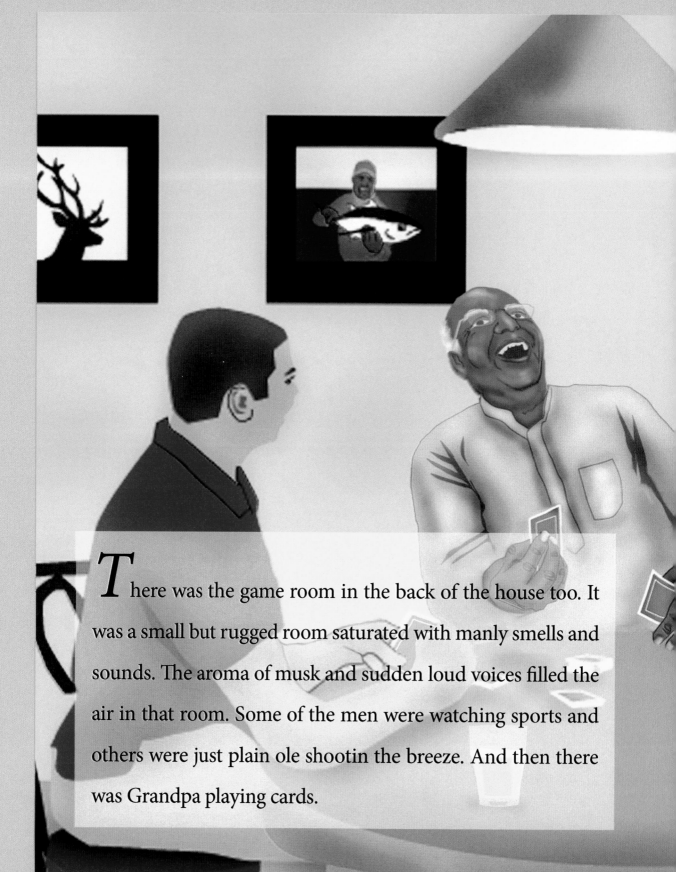

There was the game room in the back of the house too. It was a small but rugged room saturated with manly smells and sounds. The aroma of musk and sudden loud voices filled the air in that room. Some of the men were watching sports and others were just plain ole shootin the breeze. And then there was Grandpa playing cards.

14

Grandpa and his partner just did a clean sweep in the card game spades on the other team. Grandpa was as wise as an old owl and boy was he lots of fun to be around; and he was a great story teller too. Jasmine loved to be around Grandpa. He had such a great laugh that it would have been hard not to laugh with him. He also loved his ice cream. He loved it so much that everyone started calling him Grand Papa Ice Cream.

*I*n every room of the house there was a special kind of bonding going on and the love that was present would always be cherished.

Last but certainly not least was the huddle of women immersed in the festivities of the kitchen. Cakes were cooking in the oven.

The hot grease was cracklin as Aunt Millie's chicken fried on the stove. A piece of Aunt Millie's fried chicken could cure any ailment, and the "Best Cook in the Hood" plaque hung over the stove. With the smell of home cooked food, especially a freshly baked cake, life could not be any better.

That very quaint kitchen was filled with laughter, storytelling, old school R&B music, and popping beans. It was a time to practice tradition and to bond with young and old alike. It was also an honor and even a rite of passage that was important to pass down.

The women broke, peeled, snapped and popped those beans in concert with the sounds of joy and love that flooded the house. As different family members shared memories of what seemed like simpler times, Jasmine quickly chimed in and shared how Uncle Pete had got her dressed for school one day and fixed her hair so tight that she cried all day long. There was also the story about who was given the prized peach cobbler recipe that Uncle Timmy kept only in his head. And the story about how one of the cousins was always ready to dance and sing to James Brown music.

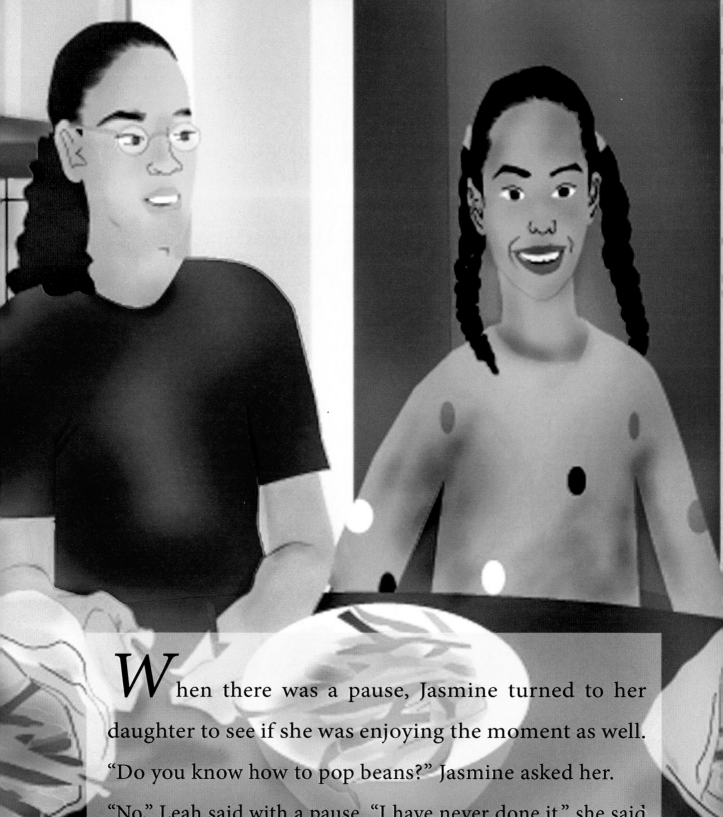

When there was a pause, Jasmine turned to her daughter to see if she was enjoying the moment as well. "Do you know how to pop beans?" Jasmine asked her. "No," Leah said with a pause. "I have never done it," she said as she continued texting her friends on her cell phone.

Leah was almost twelve years old and she didn't know how to pop beans. Immediately Jasmine called for her to come to the table, but Leah pretended not to hear her and eased back into her cell phone.

22

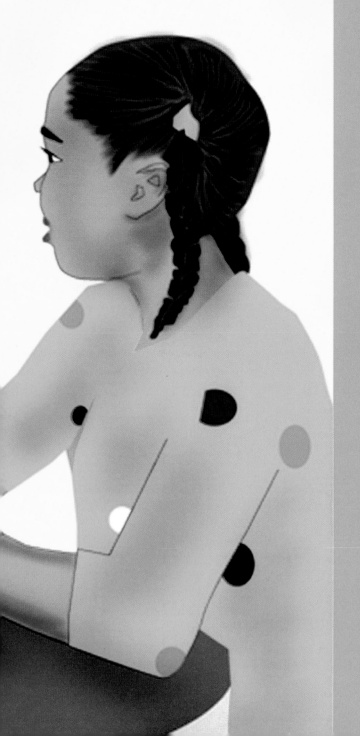

As ten year old cousin Joy walked in the room, Jasmine asked, "Has your mom ever taught you how to pop green beans?"

"Oh, yes, Cousin Jasmine," Joy said. "I remember doing that often with mommy," she replied.

Jasmine began to think about how she had missed passing down this family tradition to her own daughter. She knew her daughter had learned many other valuable things from her like, how to pray, how to clean and how to read, but teaching her how to pop beans seemed to have been absent from the list.

Suddenly a splash of water from the boiling pot hit the stove where Aunt Millie was standing. The sizzling sound of water brought Jasmine back to the kitchen and bean popping. It occurred to Jasmine, 'I can't let this tradition slip past my daughter'.

So Jasmine yelled out, "Leah! Put down that cell phone, come sit next to me and let's pop these beans. I've got a great story to tell you."

The End.

Coloring Pages

There were clusters of family in every area of the house. Aunt Maggie was in the living room with children gathered around her listening to the amazing way she told the great stories of the bible.

30

A piece of Aunt Millie's fried chicken could cure any ailment, and the "Best Cook in the Hood" plaque hung over the stove.

There were rambunctious boys playing soccer. And of course there were lots of towering teens all huddled together - talking their lingo, laughing and sharing what happened on the latest episode of the cable TV shows.

That very quaint kitchen was filled with laughter, storytelling, old school R&B music, and popping beans. It was a time to practice tradition and to bond with young and old alike. It was also an honor and even a rite of passage that was important to pass down.

Jasmine began to think about how she had missed passing down this family

tradition to her own daughter.

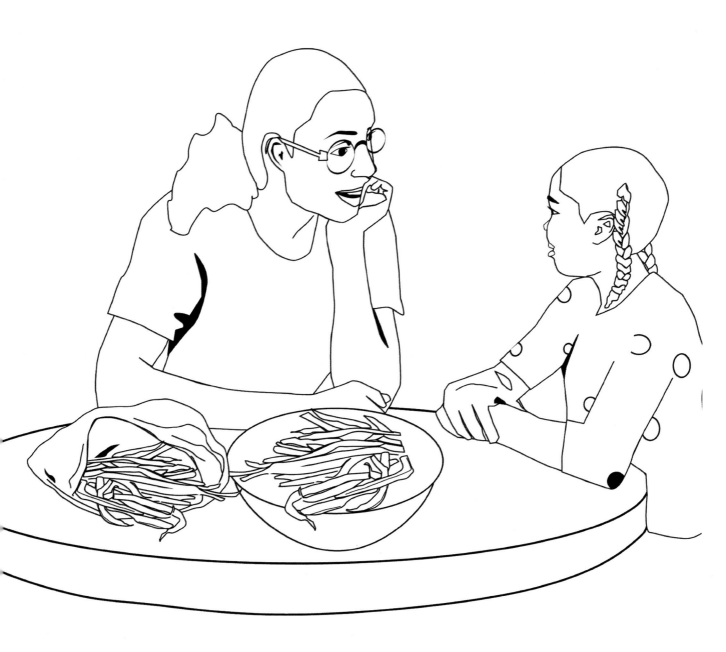

As ten year old cousin Joy walked in the room, Jasmine asked, "Has your mom

ever taught you how to pop green beans?"

So Jasmine yelled out, "Leah! Put down that cell phone, come sit next to me and let's pop these beans. I've got a great story to tell you."

Made in the USA
Middletown, DE
06 December 2021